CHRISTMAS STORY
NOTE SPELLER

by Wesley Schaum

**Twenty Stories Based on
Christmas Legends and Traditions
from Around the World**

SCHAUM PUBLICATIONS, INC.

10235 N. Port Washington Rd.   Mequon, WI 53092

©Copyright 1966 by Schaum Publications, Inc., Mequon, Wisconsin
International Copyright Secured   All Rights Reserved
Printed in U.S.A.

11-75
BP-23

Foreword

This book is designed to help students improve their sight-reading and note identification. The stories are based on Christmas legends and traditions from around the world.

To get maximum effectiveness of this speller as a note-reading aid, it is intended that each page be used as follows:

First — Pupil reads each story aloud
(This must be done *before* the letter names are written in)

Second — Pupil writes in letter names

Third — Pupil plays all of the notes at the piano

It is suggested that when a page is assigned, the student first do the written work and then practice the assigned page at the piano as part of his daily practice routine.

This speller gives equal emphasis to treble and bass notes. The reading range includes all notes in the treble and bass staffs above and below middle C. There are no leger lines or accidentals. A mixture of different note values is used to simulate an actual reading situation.

Index

Grotto of Bethlehem

Dinner on Straw

(POLAND)

In pr - -par - -tion -or the Christmas eve-

-st in Poland, a l- -yer of straw is put un- -r-

n- -th the t- -l- -loth -ore the -ishes are set in

pl- . Str- -w is also s- -ttered -out the -loor.

This serves as a r- -min- -r that Jesus h- straw -or

a when he was -orn. An extra pl- is set at the

t- -le for the Christ Child who is -liev- to

present in spirit. Everyone there is provi- with a sm- -ll

w- -r which has -n blessed by a priest. At the start of the

m- -l, the w- -rs are -roken and exchan-

as a symbol of p- and -rien- -ship.

Gift Detective

(HOLLAND)

Feast for Animals

(NORWAY)

Santa's Problem

(BRAZIL)

Holly Wreaths
(IRELAND)

Summer Christmas
(AFRICA)
At Christmas time in -ri- , it is the mi- -le o-
summer! This is true of all -ountries south of the -qu- -tor,
where the s- -sons are rev- -rs- . A -mily
o- -ten serves Christmas -inn- -r out- -oors on a
t- -le set up in -ront of their home. Many -ri- -ns
-nnot -or- to -ive -i- -ts
to -h other. However, everyone tries very h- -r- to save
so they -n -rin- - orwar -
a sm- -ll o- -rin- in honor of the Holy
-urin- the Christmas -hur- -h service.

Christmas Ghosts

(GREECE)

-urin- the tw- -lve -ys -ter Christmas, p- -ople in Gr- -lieve they must -r- -ul to avoi- -hosts. -ire, lou- noises and strong o- -ors are thou- -ht to goo- prot- -tion. For this r- -son, the -irepl- is kept -laze with a hu- log which burns -y and night. S- -lt, thistle, aspar- -us and old l- -ther shoes are thrown into the -ire to make nois- -s and sm- -lls. On the twel- -th

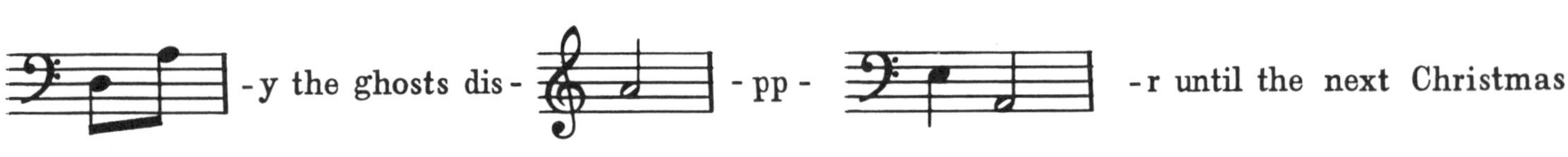

-y the ghosts dis- -pp- -r until the next Christmas.

Sailor's Salvation

(GREECE)

The Pinata

(MEXICO)

-hil- -ren take turns tryin- to -r- -k
open the pin- -t- with a sti- -k -out the
siz - of a -se- -ll -t. To make
it more -un, the pinata is hun- -ove their h- -s.
-h -hil- is -lin- -ol-
and spun -roun- thr- times - ore
trying to hit the pin- -ta. On- it is -rok-
-n open, everyone s- -ram- -les to
pi- -k up the -n- -y, -ruit and
sm- -ll pr- -sents th- -t were insi- .

Mistletoe Magic

St. Nicholas Eve

(HOLLAND)

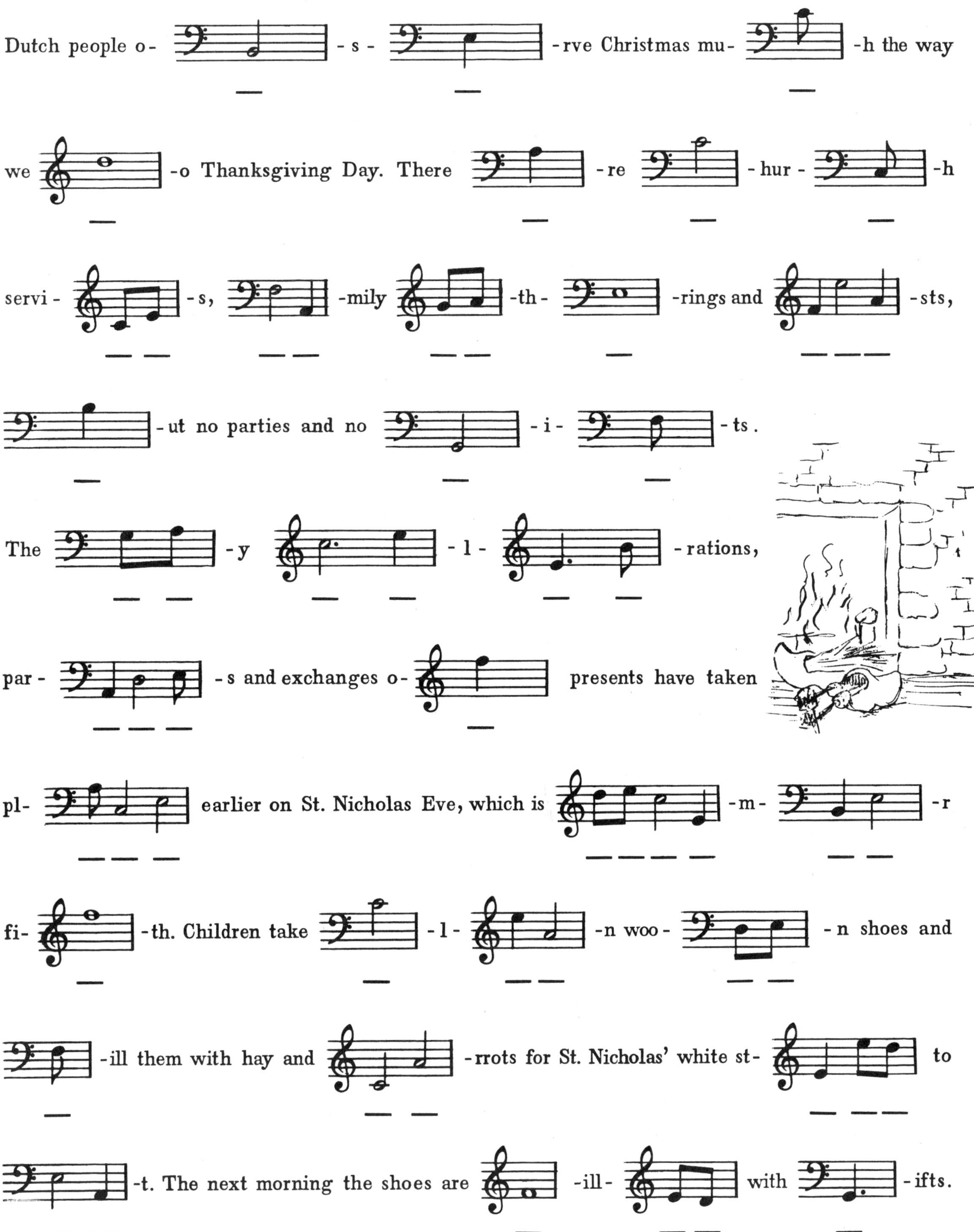

Christmas Seal Story

(DENMARK)

Trees of Long Ago

Manger Scenes
(ITALY)

Gifts from Three Kings

Trees by Candlelight

(GERMANY)

Tropical Christmas
(PHILIPPINE ISLANDS)

Tale of a Stocking

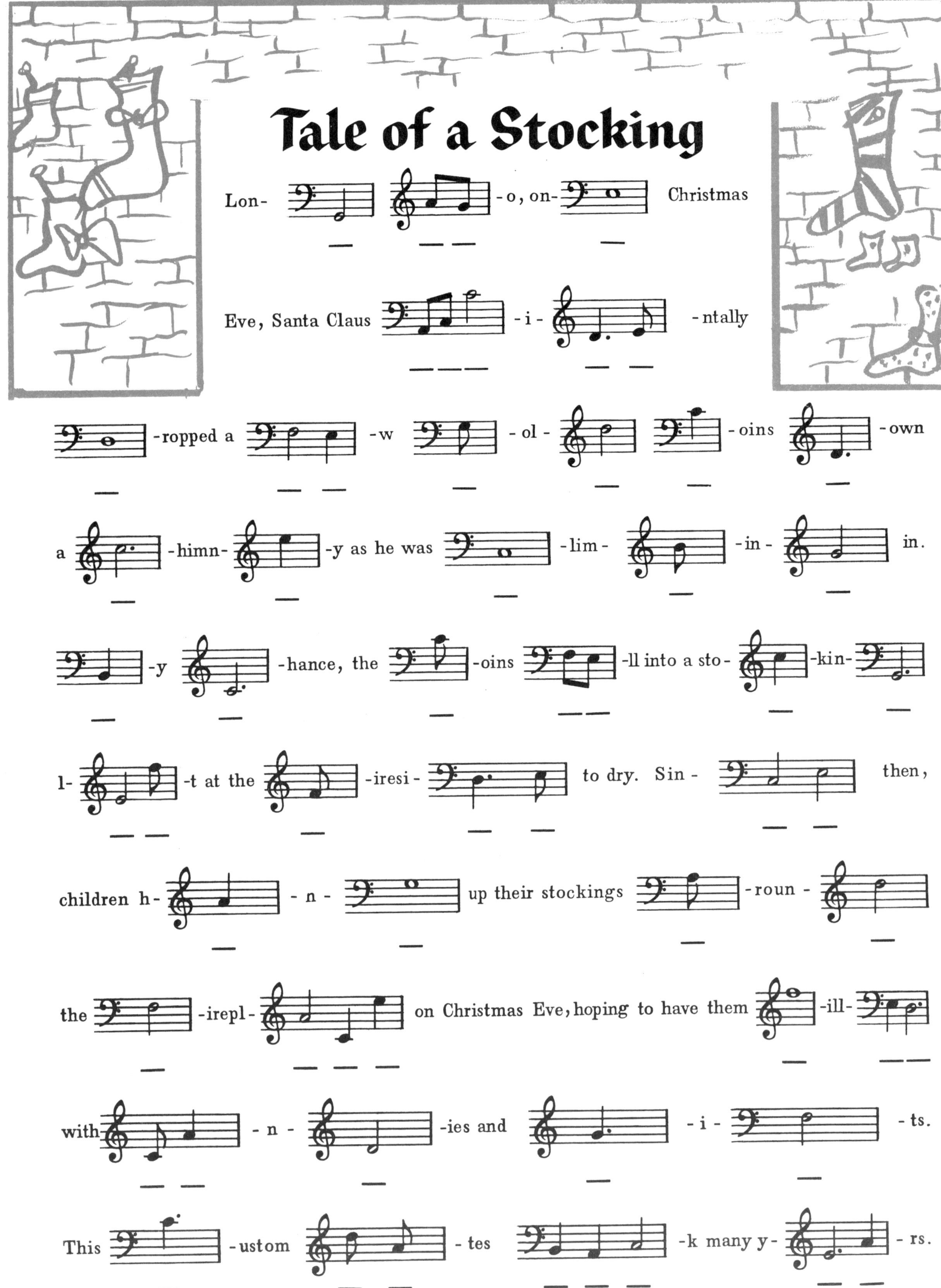

First Christmas Card

(ENGLAND)

Successful Schaum Sheet Music

This is a Partial List — Showing Level 1 through Level 2

🖐 = 5 Finger Position   * = Big Notes   • = Original Form   ✓ = Chord Symbols

LEVEL

ACTION SOLOS
52-25 *• BUBBLE BLUES ....Weston 1
55-20 * POGO STICK CHOP (Based on "Chop Sticks") *Schaum* 2
55-26 • WATER SLIDE (Staccato) ....Payne 2

ANIMALS and BIRDS
52-16 *• BUSY WOODPECKER 🖐 (Staccato) ....Cahn 1
52-36 • DINOSAUR LAND ....Schaum 1
55-54 • EQUESTRIAN PROCESSION ....Cahn 2
52-38 • KANGAROO HOP 🖐 ....Polk 1

BOOGIE
55-07 *• COOL SCHOOL (Boogie Style) ....Schaum 2

BOTH HANDS in TREBLE CLEF
52-27 • JOYOUS BELLS 🖐 (with Duet Accomp.) ....Cahn 1
55-56 • MUSIC BOX LULLABY ....Levin 2
55-44 • MYSTICAL ETUDE (Staccato) ....Cahn 2

CHRISTMAS
70-10 * IT CAME UPON THE MIDNIGHT CLEAR .. Trad. 1
81-06 LITTLE DRUMMER BOY, The .... Arr. Schaum 1
81-07 SANTA CLAUS IS COMIN' TO TOWN Arr. Schaum 1
70-02 TWELVE DAYS of CHRISTMAS ...... All 12 Verses 1
70-01 * WHAT CHILD IS THIS? ("Greensleeves") . ..... Trad. 1

CIRCUS
55-39 • CIRCUS PONIES ....Leach 2
55-58 • CLOWN WALTZ ....Kitchen 2
55-53 • RINGMASTER'S MARCH ....Cahn 2

CLASSICS
52-09 * Beethoven . SONG of JOY ("Ode To Joy" from 9th Symph.) 1
52-37 Grieg ...... In the HALL of the MOUNTAIN KING 1
52-12 ✓ Handel .... HALLELUJAH CHORUS (Easy Edition) 1
55-30 Mozart MOZART'S ROMANCE ("A Little Night Music") 2
55-45 Pachelbel ....PACHELBEL'S CANON (Easy Edition) 2
52-35 Rossini ....WILLIAM TELL MARCH 1

COUNTRY/WESTERN
55-35 DAGGER DANCE ("Land of Sky Blue Waters") ... Herbert 2
52-06 *• PONY RIDE 🖐 ....McCreary 1

DESCRIPTIVE MUSIC
52-39 • ANCIENT PAGODA ....Biel 1
52-43 *• BE A STAR 🖐 ....Rita 1
55-47 • DOMINOES ....Cahn 2
52-49 • GLIDING ....Rita 1
52-32 *• GLIDING ON THE WIND ....Hampton 1
52-44 *• GOING BY, MERRILY ....Rita 1
55-49 • IN A FAR OFF TIME & PLACE .... Revezoulis 2
52-42 *• IT'S FUN TO LEARN 🖐 ....Rita 1
52-40 • JOLLY LEPRECHAUN ....Revezoulis 1
52-46 • JUST IMAGINE IT..............................Rita 1
55-51 • PEACEFUL INTERLUDE ....Holmes 2
52-21 ✓ SCHOOL DAYS ....Edwards 1
55-42 • SUNSET SERENADE ....Levin 2

DUET (1 Piano, 4 Hands)
71-02 PARADE of the TOY SOLDIERS ....Jessel 1
71-07 HARK the HERALD ANGELS SING ... Traditional 2

HALLOWEEN
55-40 *• GALLOPING GHOSTS (Minor Key) Weston/Schaum 2
55-57 *• TRICK OR TREAT PARADE ....Rita 2
52-15 *• SPOOK HOUSE (L. H. Melody) ....Schaum 1
52-20 *• SPUNKY SPOOKS (Both Hands in Bass) ....Weston 1

LEVEL

JAZZ STYLE
55-48 • DUDE ....Weston 2

LEFT HAND MELODY
52-22 • KNOCKING AT MY DOOR 🖐 ....Schaum 1
55-50 • SCOTTISH SKETCH ....Holmes 2

MARCHES
52-34 • FANFARE ....King 1
55-06 PARADE of the TOY SOLDIERS ....Jessel 2

MINOR KEY
55-52 • DREAM CATCHER ....Holmes 2
52-28 • SECRET AGENT ....Weston 1

MOVIE THEME
80-01 STAR WARS (Main Title) ....Williams 2

PATRIOTIC
52-47 AMERICA ....Traditional 1
55-14 AMERICA THE BEAUTIFUL ....Ward 2
55-63 LIBERTY BELL MARCH ....Sousa 2
55-41 MARINE'S HYMN ....Traditional 2
55-61 STARS and STRIPES FOREVER (Easy) ..... Sousa 2
55-62 STAR SPANGLED BANNER (Easy) ....Smith 2

RAGTIME
55-21 *✓ ENTERTAINER (Easy Version) ....Joplin 2
55-55 • RICKETY RAG ....Schaum 2

SACRED
52-50 AMAZING GRACE ....Arr. W. Schaum 1
55-25 *✓ HOW GREAT THOU ART ..... Swedish Folk Melody 2

SPORTS/LEISURE
55-64 • CHA-CHA-CHA ....Leach 2
52-10 *• CHEERLEADER ....Plank 1
52-45 *• DAD'S DUNE BUGGY ....Turner 1
52-18 *• JOGGING TRAIL 🖐 (Minor Key) ....Payne 1
55-43 • ROLLER BLADES ....Schaum 2
52-41 • SKI TRAILS ....King 1
55-28 ✓ TAKE ME OUT TO THE BALL GAME . Von Tilzer 2
52-48 • TRAMPOLINE ....Revezoulis 1

SPRINGTIME
55-18 *• FAWN'S LULLABY ....Masson 2
52-04 * SPRING, SWEET SPRING ....Lincke 1
52-31 *• TREES IN THE BREEZE....................Hampton 1

STACCATO
55-23 *• FRISKY FROG (Both Hands in Treble) ....Cahn 2
52-33 • HOPSCOTCH ....Hampton 1
52-11 *• WINDSHIELD WIPER ROCK (Staccato) ......Noblitt 1

THANKSGIVING
52-24 *• PERKY TURKEY ....Weston 1
55-12 THANKSGIVING SCENE .. Medley of 4 Hymns 2

WALTZES
52-30 • OPUS ONE ....Cahn 1